Tucholsky Wagner Zola Scott Sydow Freud Schlegel
Turgenev Wallace Fonatne
Twain Walther von der Vogelweide Fouqué Friedrich II. von Preußen
Weber Freiligrath
Kant Ernst Frey
Fechner Fichte Weiße Rose von Fallersleben Richthofen Frommel
Hölderlin
Engels Fielding Eichendorff Tacitus Dumas
Fehrs Faber Flaubert
Eliasberg Ebner Eschenbach
Feuerbach Maximilian I. von Habsburg Fock Eliot Zweig
Ewald Vergil
Goethe Elisabeth von Österreich London
Mendelssohn Balzac Shakespeare Dostojewski Ganghofer
Lichtenberg Rathenau Doyle Gjellerup
Trackl Stevenson Hambruch
Mommsen Tolstoi Lenz Droste-Hülshoff
Thoma Hanrieder
von Arnim Hägele Hauff Humboldt
Dach Verne
Reuter Rousseau Hagen Hauptmann Gautier
Karrillon Garschin
Defoe Hebbel Baudelaire
Damaschke Descartes
Hegel Kussmaul Herder
Wolfram von Eschenbach Dickens Schopenhauer Rilke George
Bronner Darwin Melville Grimm Jerome
Campe Horváth Aristoteles Bebel Proust
Voltaire Federer Herodot
Bismarck Vigny Barlach Heine
Gengenbach
Storm Casanova Tersteegen Grillparzer Georgy
Chamberlain Lessing Langbein Gilm Gryphius
Brentano Lafontaine
Claudius Schiller Kralik Iffland Sokrates
Strachwitz Bellamy Schilling
Katharina II. von Rußland Gerstäcker Raabe Gibbon Tschechow
Löns Hesse Hoffmann Gogol Wilde Gleim Vulpius
Luther Heym Hofmannsthal Morgenstern
Roth Klee Hölty Goedicke
Heyse Klopstock Kleist
Luxemburg Puschkin Homer Mörike Musil
La Roche Horaz
Machiavelli Kierkegaard Kraft Kraus
Navarra Aurel Musset Moltke
Nestroy Marie de France Lamprecht Kind Kirchhoff Hugo
Laotse Ipsen Liebknecht
Nietzsche Nansen Ringelnatz
Marx Lassalle Gorki Klett Leibniz
von Ossietzky May vom Stein Lawrence Irving
Petalozzi Knigge
Platon Kafka
Sachs Pückler Michelangelo Kock
Poe Liebermann Korolenko
de Sade Praetorius Mistral Zetkin

The publishing house tredition has created the series **TREDITION CLASSICS**. It contains classical literature works from over two thousand years. Most of these titles have been out of print and off the bookstore shelves for decades.

The book series is intended to preserve the cultural legacy and to promote the timeless works of classical literature. As a reader of a **TREDITION CLASSICS** book, the reader supports the mission to save many of the amazing works of world literature from oblivion.

The symbol of **TREDITION CLASSICS** is Johannes Gutenberg (1400 – 1468), the inventor of movable type printing.

With the series, tredition intends to make thousands of international literature classics available in printed format again – worldwide.

All books are available at book retailers worldwide in paperback and in hardcover. For more information please visit: www.tredition.com

tredition was established in 2006 by Sandra Latusseck and Soenke Schulz. Based in Hamburg, Germany, tredition offers publishing solutions to authors and publishing houses, combined with worldwide distribution of printed and digital book content. tredition is uniquely positioned to enable authors and publishing houses to create books on their own terms and without conventional manufacturing risks.

For more information please visit: www.tredition.com

The Boer in Peace and War

Arthur M. Mann

Imprint

This book is part of the TREDITION CLASSICS series.

Author: Arthur M. Mann
Cover design: toepferschumann, Berlin (Germany)

Publisher: tredition GmbH, Hamburg (Germany)
ISBN: 978-3-8491-8468-1

www.tredition.com
www.tredition.de

Boer Mounted Police.ToList

TABLE OF CONTENTS

LIST OF ILLUSTRATIONS

THE BOER IN PEACE AND WAR

CHAPTER I ToC

A Boer may know you, but it will take you some time to know him, and when a certain stage in your acquaintance is reached, you may begin to wonder whether his real nature is penetrable at all. His ways are not the ways of other people: he is suspicious, distant, and he does not care to show his hand—unless, of course, there is some pecuniary advantage to be gained. He is invariably on the alert for advantages of that description.

His suspicious nature has probably been handed down to him from preceding generations. When he first set foot in South Africa he was naturally chary concerning the native population. He had to deal firmly with Bushmen, and the latter certainly proved a source of continual trouble. The Boer set himself a difficult task when he undertook to instil fear, obedience, and submission into the hearts of these barbarians—a task that could only be faced by men of firm determination and unlimited self-confidence.

These characteristics have always inspired the Boer, and although he may often have been the object of derision, it is to his credit that the predominant qualities mentioned have enabled him to pull through the miry clay. Without these qualities, it is patent that the little band which landed at the Cape long years ago would have succumbed before the conflicting forces which then existed. And as succeeding years passed on, and the sun still shone upon the heads of the pioneers, it is worthy to note that, despite the difficulties which continually presented themselves, the little band multiplied, prospered, and evolved an ensample not too mean to contemplate.

The Boer cannot be charged with any incapacity where the mere treatment of natives is concerned; he can manage that business perfectly. In the first place, he does not make the too common mistake of allowing the black populace to insert the thin end of the wedge.

This is a mistake too often fraught with serious results, and the Boer knows it. A native, no matter if he be Swazi, Zulu, Basuto, or any other nationality, will always take advantage where such is offered, and he will follow it up with enough persistence to warrant ultimate success. In Natal, at the present time, this mistake is very apparent, and, in consequence, one very seldom encounters a native who is content to attire himself in any other manner than that adopted by his master. He demands decent clothing, and, if possible, it must be new and fashionable. I have known cases where a 'boy' has been presented with a respectable suit of clothes a little too small for him, and it is unnecessary to add that he disposed of that suit. People who have hitherto allowed their children to put their pennies in the Sunday School Mission box, will perhaps hesitate to continue supporting the 'poor, down-trodden native' when they learn that he is so fastidious, and perhaps, after all, their spare coppers might be assigned to a more deserving cause.

The Boer does not treat his black servants in any such fashion — he knows better. He puts them on a sound footing to begin with, and he leads them to understand that they must remain there.

This method of treatment where the natives are concerned has, to a great extent, insured the progress of the Boer in South Africa. He has laid down certain laws at the outset, and he has rigidly adhered to those laws. He employs a different method of treatment from that which is attributed to the Natal farmer and others who employ native servants. He has never allowed his original attitude towards natives to become compatible with the British idea; he prefers still to look upon them as slaves, although he is perforce required to regard them as servants. The difficulty in Natal with regard to the rapidly increasing native populace, and how to deal effectually with the question, might have arisen in the Orange Free State, for instance, were it not for the fact that the native, in comparison with the white population, is small. By a Law passed in the Volksraad some few years ago, it became compulsory for farmers to allow only a limited number of native families to remain on the farms. This created considerable dissatisfaction among both farmers and natives, and the result was that native labour approached the inadequate in a very short time. Hundreds of native families left the State, and although the Law ultimately admitted of a wider interpretation, the native populace has not materially increased. The present attitude of natives in the towns is not altogether satisfactory since the passing of this Law. Labour being scarce, they are inclined to take up an independent attitude, which, if fraught with little danger, is at least calculated to produce a certain amount of friction between white and black. Added to this, there is the fact that the education of natives, which is becoming more general, undoubtedly assists the growth of this independence. The Boer farmers in this connection adhere to their pristine view of the matter, namely, that educating natives amounts to casting pearls before swine; and although this does not tend to encourage the work of the missionary, there may possibly be a certain amount of truth in it.

Before the arrival of British subjects at the Cape, the Boer had it all his own way. He looked upon himself as practically the ruler of the country, and it was not natural that he should look with favour upon the advent of a probable rival. He lived peacefully in a way — that is, when he was not in open conflict with the natives. He killed his game and cooked it and ate it heartily, and he enjoyed a measure of happiness. He had found a home; the free-and-easy life suited him; and if he was not possessed of riches (which would have been of little value to him then), he had, at least, health and strength and an abundance of daily food.

But one day the now accursed Englishman crossed his path, and that made a considerable difference. He perhaps wondered why the English came there at all, when he was just beginning to develop a great country. But he did not, of course, know then what he knows now, namely, that the English are insatiable land-grabbers! He looked upon their advent more in the light of a huge slice of impertinence. He knew also that it was dangerous to meddle or contend with them, so he merely looked on with a suspicious eye. He watched their every movement, and he also very probably looked for the day of their departure. But they did not depart; they had come to stay.

The Boer did not like his English neighbours from the start; there was far too much of the go-ahead persuasion about them. He wanted to jog along quietly and cautiously, and he very naturally resented the presence of people in whom the desire for progression was strong. So long as the Boer was left to himself he was not aware of his own tardiness. He was very much in the position of a cyclist on the track; it needed a 'pacer' to show how slowly he was travelling. The 'pacer' in this instance brought with him no commendation in the eyes of the Boer; he merely created suspicion and ill-feeling, which ultimately developed into rancour.

When suspicion lays hold of a man it invariably changes the whole of that man's character. It did so in the case of the Boer. It debarred any chance of reconciliation with the English for the future. The Boer does not know the meaning of compromise, and if he did, it would go against his grain to entertain it. His nature is stubborn; he cannot bring himself to look at a question from any other view-point than his own. He will argue a point for hours, and although he may be in the wrong, it is a moral impossibility to convince him that he is not in the right. His consummate ignorance may largely account for this; but even semi-educated Boers are not much better in this respect.

The Boer makes an excellent pioneer, and when he found that the English ideas were not compatible with his own, he decided to move farther north. That is another of his characteristics—independence. He is not only independent to a degree, he is sensitive; and when he discovers by accident that he is a much-aggrieved party, his indignation does not usually take a violent form—he simply clears out. He may be somewhat different where the Transvaal is concerned—he may be indignant, but he has no intention in this instance of adopting the procedure of his forefathers. The latter had not yet dropped into an inheritance glittering with gold; they were merely agriculturists, and they desired pastures of their own. Some of them found desirable pastures in the barren wastes of the Free State, and subsequently the majority wended their way to the Transvaal.

It is not, of course, my intention to reiterate history. History is good enough when it is new, but I should only be covering ground which is already familiar to most readers. My purpose is to present glimpses of the Boer as he is to-day.

CHAPTER IIToC

The Boers are very much like the Scotch—they are clannish. Every Boer has a solid belief in himself, to begin with, and every Boer has a profound belief in his brother. This characteristic has many advantages: it not only welds a people together, it is a sufficient guarantee of success in times of trouble and difficulty, and it has stood the Boer in good stead. He likes to tell you that no difficulty is insurmountable in his eyes—nay, further, he does not believe in the existence of any difficulty which he is not competent to overcome. Rumours of trouble with natives do not appal him, because he knows before he slings his gun over his shoulder that he is going forth to inflict due punishment upon the insurgents. He does not in any instance entertain the thought of a repulse. He marches to the front with a firm, determined step, and he does not rest until he has conclusively settled the matter.

The march to the front is a sort of family concern. I have tried occasionally to unravel the relations of the numerous families in certain districts, but it seems to me that the complications are too great to admit of analysis. For instance, it will be found that the family of Wessels is closely allied to the family of Odendaals, and the Odendaals, on the other hand, are related to the De Jagers. This kind of thing worries and tantalizes a man, and the only safe conclusion to arrive at is that the entire nation is linked together in some way or other by family ties. This may account for the fact that it is seldom necessary to introduce one Boer to another—they are very well acquainted without such formalities; if they are not, they very soon strike up an acquaintance.

Of course there are exceptions, and I remember one in particular. The instance I refer to occurred in a store. One of the gentlemen in question was leaning heavily against the counter, and one could observe at a glance that he, at least, had a good opinion of himself. Presently Boer number two entered. He was small in stature, like the other man, but there was a note of uncertainty about him which seemed to betoken that his opinion of himself did not measure up in proportion to that of the other Boer. Number two looked about him a bit, and occasionally directed a furtive glance at number one, who, on the other hand, stolidly regarded the array of goods spread out before him. Number two seemed to have settled the question in his own mind at last, for he approached the other party and held out his hand.

'I am Britz,' he said laconically, as the other touched the outstretched hand indifferently.

'Ja!' said number one; 'I am Papenfus.'

The conversation ended here, and number two made a silent departure.

Waggons Bringing Wool To Early Morning Market (Johannesburg).ToList

The preliminary salutations of another pair of Boers are probably as interesting. It was during a prolonged drought, and both gentlemen had evidently experienced a difficulty in finding a sufficiency of water for the purposes of ablution. They had not met for a number of years, but the recognition was mutual.

'Almachtig, Gert, you are still as ugly as ever!'

'Ja!' replied the other readily; 'and you are still alive with that face!'

The Boer is coarse in his conversation, although he prefers to regard it as wit. He likes to participate in a conversation bristling with this sort of wit, but when you come to tell him a really good thing, he fails entirely to grasp the point, and your joke falls flat, resulting usually in a painful silence.

He is also very chary of complications in the handling of money. He brings his wool into town once, and sometimes twice, a year, and that staple comprises the current coin of the country. His clip is weighed off in due course, and he proceeds to the store and sits down while the clerk figures up the amount. You may be foolish enough to ask him if he will buy a plough or a bag of coffee, but he continues to smoke hard and expectorate all over the floor without giving a definite reply. He wants to handle the money first, and then he will arrange about his purchases. Within half an hour he will probably have in his pocket two or three hundred golden sovereigns (he does not look upon bank-notes with favour; he wants something hard and substantial), and he will at once proceed to the matter of buying. At the end of the day his waggon is loaded up with a variety of household and agricultural necessities, for which he has paid, say, £150 of the money received for his wool. This is his way of doing things, and he thinks it is the right one.

During the Boer War of 1880 merchants in the Free State had a bad time of it. The Boers were, of course, very much excited, and the English merchant was looked upon scornfully and contemptuously. One Boer had already drawn up a memorandum of what he considered should be the *modus operandi* in dealing with the storekeepers. Two or three were to be hanged, and the others were to be tied up in front of their own buildings and shot down like crows. That was in Harrismith.

The Boer has not much to boast of in the matter of brains, but what he does possess he is careful not to abuse. A man can abuse his brains in many ways—by taking to strong drink, for instance. I have been among Boers for some years, and I can honestly say that I never yet saw a Boer the worse for drink. He may indulge occasionally, but he very seldom carries the practice to excess. When he does take it he likes it strong—as strong as he can get it. He scorns the idea of mixing it in water. He reckons that he did not go to the canteen or hotel to pay for water. He wants the full value of his money, and he takes it.

I have said that the Boer is suspicious; he is likewise jealous by nature. If there happens to be rinderpest on the next farm to his, he is never contented until he gets his full share. He does not mind if the visitation plays extreme havoc among his stock so long as he is not left in the lurch. I remember some time ago hearing of a Boer who had decided to build a large dwelling-house on his farm in place of the wretched little building he and his family had hitherto occupied. This Boer had made some money, and contact with English people in the towns had resulted in more advanced ideas. He determined, therefore, to spare no expense on this new project—he even included a bath-room. The building was scarcely completed, when about a dozen Boers, who were also capitalists in a way, immediately set about making arrangements for similar structures. This form of jealousy is, of course, good where trade is concerned.

If the Boer is nothing else, he is at least talked about. I say nothing else advisedly, because he is nothing else. In his own country he is nothing, and out of it he is less, if that were possible. It may seem out of place on the part of a Scotsman to make such an assertion, because a Scotsman (and a Yorkshireman, too, by the way) is, in the eyes of the Boer, a friendly being, and far removed above a mere Englishman. A Boer will give a Scotsman the best in the house, and put up his horse comfortably, but an Englishman in the same circumstances fares differently. It is, of course, unnecessary to say that while a Scotsman makes no objection to exceptional hospitality, his views of the Boer do not differ materially from those of any other person of whatever nationality. He drinks the Boer's coffee, and shakes hands with him and all his family, but there may be, and usually is, a great deal of deception mixed up with such extreme good-feeling. I could never understand, nor has it been explained to me, why the Boer is so partial towards Scotsmen, unless it be that a great many Scotch words resemble words in the Dutch language. Perhaps that may in some degree account for it, although I do not think there is anything to be proud of on the Scottish side.

A Boer Homestead.ToList

It is necessary to reside in the Boer Republics to place one in the position of knowing something of the Boer, and a mere fortnight won't do it. Of course, there are Boers and Boers, as there are Englishmen and Englishmen. There are Boers who are competent to rank with any English gentleman, and whose education and abilities are of no mean order. Unfortunately, however, these are altogether in the minority.

The Boers are all farmers, and, according to their own statements, a poverty-stricken people. They plead poverty before an English merchant because they fancy it will have the effect of reducing prices. Fortunately, the merchants possess rather an accurate knowledge of such customers, and in consequence they lose nothing. One would as soon believe the generality of Boers, as walk into the shaft of a coal mine. He has a reputation for lying, and he never brings discredit upon that reputation. When he lies, which, on an average, is every alternate time he opens his mouth, he does so with great enthusiasm, and the while he is delivering one lie, he is carefully considering the next. When he can't think of any more lies, he starts on the truth, but in this he is a decided failure. He is afraid of being found out. For instance, a merchant will approach a Boer respecting an overdue account. The Boer will at once plead poverty, and speculate on how he can possibly manage to liquidate his liability. If the merchant knows the ropes sufficiently (and the majority of merchants do), he will drop the subject for half an hour, at the end of which time he will ask the Boer if he wants to sell any cattle or produce, as he (the merchant) can find an outlet for either or both. The Boer's diplomacy is weak, and he falls into the trap. He has fifty cattle to dispose of; the merchant buys them, and the overdue account, with interest, is paid.

The Boers are very superstitious in a great many things. For instance, they regard locusts as a direct visitation from the Almighty. When the pest settles down upon ground occupied by Kaffirs, all the available tin cans and empty paraffin tins are requisitioned, and there is a mighty noise, that ought to frighten off any respectable locust swarm; but the Boer, when he sees them coming, goes into his house and lays hold of his Bible, and reads and prays until he thinks there ought to be some good result. The Boer is gifted with great and abiding patience (in such cases only), and, no matter if the locusts stop long enough to eat up every green blade on his farm, he will continue to study his Bible and pray. But, as I have remarked parenthetically, it is only in cases of emergency where he evinces such a display of patience and exercises such a pious disposition. When he is not praying, he is putting ten-pound stones in his bales of wool to be ready for the merchant's scales, and transacting other little matters of business of a like nature.

The Boer is not particular in the matter of cleanliness. It suits him just as well to be dirty as to be clean. It is no exaggeration to say that numbers of Boers do not wash themselves from one week's end to another; and they wear their clothes until they drop off. It is always a matter for speculation what the womenfolks do. It is certain that they do not exert themselves too much, if at all, in their own homes. They generally do all the cooking and eating in one room, and in the other end of the house you will probably find a litter of pigs, a score of hens, etc. And the one room is about as clean as the other — most people would prefer to sleep alongside the pigs and the fowls.

The most painful proceeding is to dine in such a place. Unless you are blessed with a cast-iron constitution and a stomach of the same pattern, you are not likely to survive. Usually they put down boiled meat first, after which comes the soup. The chief regret in your case is that the soup had not come first, so that you could have disposed of it right away and had something on top of it. Coffee, of course, is never forgotten, and it would be a direct insult to refuse it. Coffee is a great thing with the Boer. He would as soon be without house and home, as his bag of coffee. Before selling his wool to the merchant, almost the first thing he asks is: 'What is your price for coffee?' If a satisfactory quotation is forthcoming, he does not hesitate long in disposing of his staple, although, of course, at the highest price obtainable.

The story goes that once upon a time a Boer, whose conscience had remained dormant from his birth, came to a certain town to purchase goods in exchange for produce. One of the articles he bought was, naturally, coffee, and of that he took half a bag. While the clerk was engaged in attending to some other matters, the Boer quietly and, as he thought, unobserved, undid the cord which secured the mouth of the coffee bag, and slipped in a quarter of a hundred-weight of lead which was lying in the vicinity and which he evidently calculated on finding useful. The clerk observed this movement without betraying the fact, and when the order was completed his eye fell upon the coffee bag casually.

'Oh! wait a moment,' he remarked. 'I fancy I have forgotten to weigh that coffee.'

He weighed it over again and carefully noted down the figures in his little book, no doubt much to the chagrin of the silent Boer, who probably had not reckoned on paying for his lead in the same proportion as the cost of his coffee per pound.

On another occasion, a Boer, the extent of whose wealth was probably unknown to himself, found it necessary to dispute certain items in his account with his storekeeper. This sort of thing, by the way, is the rule and by no means the exception. It seems natural also when it is noted that the majority of Boers run twelve-monthly accounts, and by the time they come to square up, they find a difficulty in recognising some of the articles purchased eleven or twelve months previously. This particular gentleman's argument had reference to a pair of spurs, which he deposed had been given to him as a present by the manager, and his hitherto good opinion of the clerk who had charged the spurs in his account was permanently damaged. He said he wasn't a man of that sort. If he wanted to buy spurs, he could pay cash down for about fifteen thousand pairs and, in short, he could buy up all the spurs in the country! He would pay for those spurs now: he wouldn't take a pair of anything, gratis or otherwise, from that merchant as long as he lived. He would go home and put eight horses into his wagonette and drive round the country and tell all his friends about that pair of spurs, and he wouldn't rest until he had completed the task to his own satisfaction.

The book-keeper tried in vain to calm him down by presenting him with a bunch of grapes, but he only regarded the peace-offering with extreme contempt. He wanted to know what else he had been charged with, and the clerk, in conciliatory tones, proceeded to read over the several items. He came to 'one pound of tea.' That was the last straw.

'What! a pound of tea—a pound! Almachtig! Ik koop thee bij de zak (I buy tea by the bag).'

The suspicious nature of the Boer is always in evidence, although the Englishman must perforce humour it. It would be interesting to learn, for instance, how many thousands of pounds are sewn up in mattresses all over the country because the owners are chary concerning the integrity of bank-managers. They have no doubt whatever but that a bank is a paying concern (one Boer entered a bank recently and wanted to see the place where they made the money), but they would much rather keep their own money out of it, in case it should get mixed up with the earnings and savings of other people and be lost. The story runs that one old vrouw journeyed to town in her waggon one day for the express purpose of depositing £300 with the local bank, but when she found that they wanted to give her so much for keeping it (interest) instead of asking her to pay a small amount by way of compensation for taking charge of her money, she became suspicious and took her £300 back to the farm and the double grass mattress once more. It is unnecessary to state that this particular lady never trusted another banking institution.

Waggons Crossing River.ToList

And so it is with other things. When once you have aroused suspicion in the Boer—and it sleeps lightly—you can safely say good-bye to him for ever. He knows within his heart that the English are bent upon taking advantage of him, and when a man makes up his mind like that he is seldom disappointed.

There is one characteristic of the Boer which the most casual observer cannot fail to notice. It is his entire indifference to personal appearance. He likes to see his vrouw gorgeous in all the colours of the rainbow (pink and green being the favourites), and he doesn't mind if the material costs a little over ninepence a yard; but he evinces no desire to discard the suit he has himself worn for three or four years without a change. So long as it holds together, he is content to wear it, and he does not in the least mind what other people may say about it. It may be supposed that this applies exclusively to the poorer classes, but I can assure my readers that I have known it to be the case with scores of men who could well afford to wear a brand-new suit every day of the week and every month of the year. And what does this characteristic indicate? It indicates the man. He has no desire to advance beyond what he is—what his forefathers were. The latter manufactured their own clothing; they made their own shoes, and, had they been presented with a cast-off suit belonging to the Prince of Wales, they could not possibly have appreciated it, and they certainly would never have thought of wearing it. The Boer does not care to dress respectably; he prefers to finger the coin and sit down and watch the increase in his stock. He would have everything converted into stock, because that is his great ambition.

Another thing—he lacks taste. His clothes never by any chance fit him (in the eyes of more refined people), and his boots are always three sizes too large; but then he thinks he is getting more for his money. If he must needs buy boots, he takes care that he invests his money in quantity, not quality, or style.

CHAPTER IIIToC

The Boer would like to lay hands on the man who invented ploughs. Not that he has any aversion to ploughs as ploughs; he merely objects to the labour involved by the introduction of these implements into the market. He sees some sense in an ox, a sheep, a goat, and a horse. Put these animals on a bit of green veldt, and they do the rest themselves; they thrive and multiply, and enhance the position of their owner. But a plough! It means that he requires to take off his coat and stop doing nothing. The Boer would like to argue that if God had meant the soil to be disturbed by ploughs and such like, He would not have left the solution of this problem in the hands of mere inventors: He would have ordained a means whereby the soil would have of itself turned over once a year at springtime.

The Boers are a pastoral people—one can hardly say an agricultural people. They have been that sort of people from the start, and they will never change. They are used to waggons and oxen and sheep, and the waggons and oxen and sheep have got quite used to them. There is abundance of proof in the Dutch Republics to satisfy any ordinary person that a Boer, no matter if he can count his sovereigns by the million, would never dream of giving up his farm and turning country gentleman. He may take no part in the actual work (and this is not much in his line under any circumstances), but he exercises that amount of careful supervision necessary to successful farming, and continues to do so until the end. Even the members of the Volksraad, who are usually well-to-do farmers, never neglect their crops, albeit a handsome income is assured in their official capacity.

But does farming in the Dutch Republics pay? Most emphatically, No. I am not making this assertion because I have tried it myself, I am simply quoting the dictum of every Boer. I have been careful to obtain a consensus of opinion on this question for the guidance of those who may contemplate embarking upon such an unsatisfactory and dangerous undertaking. Farming does not pay. For my own satisfaction, I recently questioned a Boer with regard to his average yearly income, and he was good enough to humour me.

The value of his stock worked out as follows:

1,000 sheep	say	£ 500
100 head of cattle	"	1000
48 horses	"	480
		£1980

£ s. d.

His yearly clip averaged 10 bales	@ £10 =	100 0 0
On an average he sold:		
20 head of cattle	" £ 8 =	160 0 0
10 horses	" £10 =	100 0 0
Butter, 1,000 pounds	" 1s. =	50 0 0
Hides and skin	say	5 0 0
Horns	"	1 0 0
Mealies, 60 bags	" 12s. =	36 0 0
Forage, 5,000 bundles	" 3d. =	62 10 0
Kaffir corn, 30 bags	" 15s. =	22 10 0
Total average yearly income		£537 0 0

It must not be supposed for one moment that here we have a rich man. I am merely citing the case of a farmer who said to me: 'I'd rather be a book-keeper at twenty-pounds a month.' He had no idea that his annual income figured up to anything like £537. And yet that same man would endeavour to make a good bargain in purchasing sixpennyworth of hairpins because he considered himself a 'poor man.'

There are hundreds of farmers, more particularly in the Free State, who are unable to realize the extent of their wealth in stock or the acreage of their own farms. They brand every ox, sheep, and horse that belongs to them, and it is only by such marks that they are enabled to recognise their own property when they see it. I have known instances where hundreds of horses belonging to one man have succumbed in a single season on account of horse-sickness, and their owner regarded the loss as a mere trifle, because he knew that such a catastrophe did not materially affect his position.

Klondyke had its 'millionaires in huts,' Boerland has its millionaires in hovels. You will find farmers who are worth many thousands of pounds living in places under whose roofs a Kaffir would certainly disdain to pass the night. They possess wives and families, too, but they exhibit no desire to better their domestic surroundings. If the houses happen to include another room other than the living room, that extra room is invariably used for storing grain. The women are untidy and unprepossessing, and the children have not yet learned to appreciate stockings and shoes. It is almost paradoxical to think of human beings in a civilized country living such lives, people who have great possibilities within their reach. The children readily assimilate the habits and ways of their parents, and grow up into men and women of a like type, and so on from generation to generation. No wonder, then, that the Boers are a retrograde race.

A Boer Family.ToList

It has been made sufficiently plain that when once the Boers have acquired a country, they allow that country to rest in peace—from an agricultural point of view only. This is quite apparent when it is explained that the Free State has an estimated acreage of 7,491,500, and out of that only 75,000 acres are cultivated. This is not the fault of the country, but of the Boer himself. He has no sooner settled down on a bit of land, where there is a plentiful growth of grass to feed his stock, than he longs for pastures new, his only reason for staying where he is being that he does not want the Englishman to step into his homestead.

No exhibition of national prejudice is intended when I say that were the Dutch Republics sprinkled with a few hundred Scottish farmers, these countries would assume a more fertile and healthy aspect in two or three years. The soil is good; all that is wanted is concentrated hard work, and the countries would surprise several people — the Boers, for instance — by the extent of their agricultural wealth. There are, of course, climatic disadvantages to contend against — prolonged droughts are of common occurrence — but, as in other countries, the farmer must take the bad with the good. The great thing with the Boer is stock, and plenty of it. He does not care about anything else until the rinderpest comes.

Comparisons are odious, but let us compare the Boer with the English farmers. Should the harvests of the latter be destroyed (as in the case of an entire county of farmers in England at one time), ruin stares them in the face, showing that stock is of little moment. It is different in the case of the Boer. Take his stock away from him, and you deprive him of his daily bread. Of course, the facilities for successful cultivation in England are different from those in the Dutch Republics; at the same time, there is such a thing as irrigation, and were this resorted to more generally, and a larger area of land put under cultivation, the Boer farmer would be on a more stable footing.

A somewhat erroneous deduction has been gleaned by many people from guide-books, in which particulars are given respecting the limited extent of arable land available, but guide-book makers mostly prefer to guess at the figures rather than go to the trouble of ascertaining the truth. Without further reference to the guide-books, it is noteworthy that the possibilities of both the Transvaal and Free State, from an agricultural point of view, are greatly underestimated, the fact being that a very small proportion of arable land is cultivated at all. In a number of cases water facilities are entirely ignored.

Wool is the current coin of the country with the Boer farmers, and the merchant who is desirous of continuing his business must have a certain amount of capital behind him, because the farmer likes to see money at least once a year. Things have changed somewhat now. In the olden days it was different. It was absolutely necessary then to put down a cheque for the full amount, but the average farmer is becoming less suspicious in transactions of this nature.

The life of the merchant during the wool season is not exactly a happy one. He likes to please his customers, but he does not always succeed. The average farmer who comes in with a load of wool has the appearance of a man whose primary intention is to buy up all the stores (although he may go away with a bag of coffee only), and afterwards consider with great deliberation the question of acquiring the whole town. All this is based upon the fact that he has a load of wool for sale. The merchant would rather give him five shillings than fivepence per pound, because it would be a certain sign that the good times had arrived. No matter, however, what price the merchant offers, your average farmer can always obtain more. He does not say where; he prefers to keep that up his sleeve. He also advances by farthings and halfpence, because he is chary about entering into the intricacies of eighths. He, moreover, strongly objects to accepting a lower price than that given to his neighbour. His neighbour may be an excellent man, and he may be in possession of very good sheep, but that his wool should be more valuable is not so apparent—is, in fact, most improbable. Every farmer has implicit faith in the merits of his own particular clip, and if differences really exist, he is prepared to state emphatically that the advantage is on his side.

CHAPTER IVToC

There has been a good deal of speculation as to why the Boers are such experts with the rifle, but that is easily and naturally explained. In the first place, they know their own country, and that is a decided advantage where bare veldt is concerned. An Englishman on the same ground would make mistakes, and probably sight his rifle at 200 yards; but the Boer puts his up to 500 yards and kills his game, whilst the Englishman, with his imperfect knowledge of the country, misses it. When the Dutch first settled in South Africa, they were compelled either to shoot their dinner or go without. So they began straight away by shooting their dinner — and they have been able to shoot it ever since. In warfare, too, they know exactly how to proceed. They know that it is policy to shoot the Englishmen and save their own skins. So they get behind large stones and shoot the Englishmen. They know, further, that the best guarantee of success is to wait patiently. They know nothing about military discipline, and they don't want to know anything about it. According to their idea, this is how the crack British regiments proceed: They march up in a body — close order — and when they come within range of the Boers the commanding officer gives the following commands: 'Halt! Attention! Present! Fire!' And by the time the commanding officer has given the word 'Fire!' the Boers, comfortably stationed behind stones, have shot those regiments down! There is, perhaps, some truth in this.

But the Boer, after all, believes in peace. It suits him better to be on his farm, with a pipe in his mouth, and Kaffirs to do all the work, while he walks around his acres and finds fault. They stick to their country, and they fight for their country; but they don't like fighting much. I came across one particular Boer who had been at Majuba, and who was perfectly clear in his own mind that he did not care much about it; and he did not entertain favourably the idea of further warfare. He explained that he quietly got behind the customary stone, and shot round the corners. During the time he was thus amusing himself, the stone was struck by fifteen English bullets, and he did not calculate on waiting to see what effect number sixteen would have, so he left that stone. The Boers are always very reticent where the number of their killed is concerned. In English circles it is jocularly asserted that only one Boer was killed at Majuba, and all the other Boers went into mourning for him. It is not known, and never will be known, how many were killed at Krugersdorp by Jameson's men. There is one thing, however, which goes to prove that a good number must have succumbed on that occasion. It is rumoured that the Boers do not want any more fighting with men who shoot as straight as those comprising Jameson's Horse.

Majuba Hill.ToList

Defence in the Transvaal and Orange Free State is provided for principally by the burghers, who are liable to be called upon for active service between the ages of eighteen and sixty. The mounted police force in both Republics is comparatively small, and the permanent corps of artillery in each case is also small. The Boers do not, as a matter of fact, repose much confidence in artillery at any time, and they regard the mounted police force as valuable only in time of peace. The burghers themselves comprise the entire force. In the Free State alone there are 17,000 burghers liable to be called up on commando at a moment's notice.

The country is divided into districts, and each district is under the charge of a Commandant and a Field-cornet. The duty of the latter is to warn the burghers on receipt of instructions from his Chief, and he may also call a meeting of burghers in his district should any crisis of a serious nature be imminent. On the whole, the Field-cornet's life is not a happy one; and although he has numerous opportunities of making himself objectionable and disagreeable, he usually prefers to perform his onerous duties in a humble and unassuming spirit. In times of peace those duties are few. In the first place, he must satisfy himself that all the burghers in his district are in possession of rifles and ammunition; and in the second place, he must call the burghers together once a year for inspection. The good old times are now over when a score of burghers could with impunity produce one and the same rifle. In those days it was customary for burghers to appear for inspection when convenient to themselves, and in these circumstances it was not a difficult matter to borrow your neighbour's rifle and present it as your own. But this little game was found out, and an order was at once issued to the effect that all burghers must assemble at one particular hour. The weapons used are of different kinds, but they must all be breech-loaders. Every burgher must likewise be in possession of thirty rounds of ammunition, and in time of war the Government supply unlimited ammunition. Should the burghers be called out to action, they must supply themselves with provisions to last fourteen days. This might be difficult to carry out, but the explanation is simple. The provisions consist solely of biltong—that is, dried meat, generally venison. The sustenance contained in even an inch of this is such that the fourteen days' provision amounts to but little in bulk. It is said that if a Boer has a rifle, ammunition, and a piece of biltong in his pocket, he will fight till further orders.

It is surprising how quickly the burgher forces can be levied. This was made very apparent when Dr. Jameson marched into the country on December 29, 1895. It is also well known that news travels quickly, even in the outlying districts, and in this respect the Boers appear to be quite as remarkable as the Kaffirs.

All this military discipline might seem to be only good in itself, were it not for the fact that the Boers still retain their reputation for being good shots. Even the young men are not behind their fathers in the masterly manipulation of their rifles; in fact, while a large number of Englishmen are reputed to be born with silver spoons in their mouths, the birth-right of every Boer is undoubtedly the rifle.

Both in the Transvaal and Free State there exists a healthy spirit of rivalry between Englishman and Boer in the shooting line. Competitions are very frequently arranged; it is to the credit of the colonial Englishman that he can give a good account of himself, and at the same time hold his own against any Boer. This is fortunate, because the Boer always respects a man who can record as many bull's-eyes as himself, no matter what his nationality may be. The great opportunity the Boer had of giving vent to his contempt for the English was when the latter appeared on the battlefield in compact regiments, and afforded the best possible target for shooting at from behind the now proverbial stone.

In these times of universal political difficulties it may be interesting to survey the position of the Orange Free State now that war has actually broken out with Great Britain. There is a patriotism lurking in the breast of the Boer which would indicate that his great aim was the overthrow of the hated Englishman. It would not be advisable to quote the opinion the generality of Boers have of the poor Englishman; needless to say it is strong, emphatic, comprehensive, and by no means complimentary. Obviously the origin of such opinion concentrates in the fact that the Englishman is too persevering in other people's countries, and, moreover, shows an aptitude for developing the said countries which, in the opinion of the Boer, is altogether too progressive. It is, of course, a pity that the Englishman cannot accommodate himself to the antiquated ideas of the Boer, because if he could, he would probably exonerate himself in the Dutch eyes, and at the same time find himself away back in the eighteenth century. But in this advanced age he is too much for the Boer, and this is probably the explanation of the existing friction.

The Orange Free State has all along evinced a helping-hand where Transvaal broils have occurred. This is not surprising, considering that the Free State is governed by a Volksraad wholly in sympathy with the mighty Oom Paul. In the time of President Brand things were slightly different, although even his Volksraad held him in check and exercised its own influence. But President

Brand had sense enough to see that participation in Transvaal difficulties could in no way benefit the Free State, and, in fact, that interference was not desirable or advisable. When the previous Boer War
broke out, he intimated that no commandeering would be enforced
in the Free State, but that those burghers who chose to engage in
warfare might do so. He would take no active steps until the independence of the Free State was endangered.

His successor in office, President Reitz, was not credited with anything in particular, but it was understood that should the Volksraad decide to co-operate with the Transvaal in any instance, he
would willingly give his consent. This was confirmed when Dr.
Jameson's entrance into the Transvaal was made known. Three
districts of the Free State were promptly commandeered, and
burghers swarmed to the border.

A Boer Encampment.ToList

About the same time President Reitz vacated his office, and President Steyn is now at the head of affairs. President Steyn has now
conclusively shown his sympathy with the Transvaal, and his occa-
sional interviews with Oom Paul were presumably for the purpose
of ratifying the compact from time to time. This is confirmed by the
fact that the Volksraad some considerable time ago proclaimed that,

when hostilities broke out in the Transvaal, the burghers were to hold themselves in readiness to proceed to the border. This was not merely with the object of protecting the border, but to render assistance to those across the border, and now they have joined their neighbours in invading Natal.

The feeling amongst Englishmen in the Free State was, of course, strong, but Englishmen are not considered in the matter at all. If they are burghers of the State, they must perforce conform to the laws thereof, and fight to the death even against their own relations. If they refuse to go to the front, it is not certain what would happen.

There is another aspect of the question, and a serious one, too. When the Free State burghers were called to the border, and war was actually declared, they feared that they would return to their homes only to find that their wives and children had been murdered, their cattle stolen, and their property burnt to the ground. This new and terrible danger came from Basutoland. The Basutos have a grudge against the Boers, and they were only waiting an opportunity to wipe out that grudge for ever. They are a warlike race, they are well supplied with arms, and their horsemanship is notorious. They like the Englishman, but they look upon the Boer as something to wipe off the face of the earth. Of course, their discrimination between English and Dutch when the time comes for them to take action, if it ever does come, will not save the Englishmen in the Free State.

The Basuto question may not have escaped the notice of the Volksraad in their anxiety to assist their brethren in the Transvaal, but their action would seem to indicate that it had. Had they been wise, they would have left their sister country to settle its own affairs, and have looked nearer home for something to do; but this view, although now too late, may already have engaged their attention.

Apart from the Government of the country, it may be interesting to reflect upon the opinions of the burghers themselves, i.e., the Dutch burghers. The majority of the young men originally favoured the action of the Volksraad. They had not tasted war; they had only heard about it; and their contempt for the English race generally suggested a trial. Their enthusiasm was undoubtedly great, and the idea of lending a helping-hand to another country evidently fascinated them. But their elders have now come to look upon interference as bad policy, and they dread the possibility of handing over their possessions to the wily Basuto. The feelings of the Free State Boers towards their English friends were scarcely so vindictive as in the Transvaal, but perhaps that is because there are no gold mines in the Free State.

CHAPTER VToC

It must not be supposed that the intelligent Boer is non-existent; but, as I have said, he is in the minority. He reads the newspapers, and he has a great deal to say on both sides. He has very few personal prejudices; his whole concern is concentrated in a desire to further the progress of the country. His mind is developed; he does not regard the Englishman as an interloper; he wants 'to live and let live.'

There is, unfortunately, the other element, a most undesirable one—the Boer who is continually stirring up ill-feeling. You will find him everywhere, and he is always at it. If his own brother happened to be an educated man, he could not get on with him; his nature is despicable. President Kruger thinks that race hatred will gradually disappear, for 'wherever love dwells, prosperity must follow.' Can anyone imagine love existing in the nature of the man I have cited? President Kruger himself is an educated man, an able man in his own sphere. If he practises the art of brotherly love to the same extent that he preaches it, why does he not make some arrangement by which it would be possible to instil a portion of the sentiment into some of his erring children? Then we should have no more racial hatred to concern ourselves with; we should have instead the inspiring spectacle of a reclaimed Dutchman falling upon the neck of his English next-door neighbour and weeping.

At the same time, however, even supposing Oom Paul's influence were capable of producing such picturesque results, it would be well meantime if a little fundamental education could be introduced. This may seem impracticable at the first blush, considering that the population is so widely scattered, but no doubt there is some hidden solution. Ignorance is accountable in a great measure for the ill-feeling which exists between Dutch and English, and rancour cannot be removed until ignorance is ordered out through the back-door.

Raadzaal, Or Boer Parliament House.ToList

There is also the fact that the generality of the people exhibit little or no interest in the leaders of their Government. It is said that the perusal of biography ennobles and develops the mind. This is also the case when a man follows with interest and profit the mature reasoning and diplomatical tact of some of our present-day politicians. I say some of them, because not all of them exhibit that intellectual refinement which characterized the great Plato. Still, a great many people might acquire a tolerable education if they applied themselves to the perusal of newspapers in this way, and it is my firm belief that the Boers would benefit by such a course.

The average Boer does not know exactly the meaning of the word 'politics,' except that in most things he prefers to be conservative. He likes to move along very quietly, without any outside interference. He knows full well that he has sent his representative to Parliament, and he leaves that member severely alone. Sometimes the member calls a public meeting of his own accord, and the Boer attends that meeting, not because he is anxious to bring forward any matter affecting the welfare of his country or district, nor because the member has failed to satisfy him, but merely because he is desirous of meeting his fellow-men and discussing crops and Kaffirs and oxen and sheep and wool — in short, anything outside of politics, in which he professes no interest whatever. He is not interested in general measures for the benefit of the whole country; his attention is fully occupied with the affairs of his own particular piece of land, and so long as he himself prospers, he does not trouble about the prosperity or otherwise of his neighbours.

Oom Paul is the leading light, and should he elect to do this or that, he need exercise no discretion concerning the probable feeling of the country. He is the man at the wheel, and the crew have such implicit faith in him that he can practically steer where he wills. He may sometimes experience a little opposition in the House, but he is long-headed as well as hard-headed, and he invariably holds the trump card. He is not a Boer in the ordinary sense of the word; he is only a Boer in the sense that he smokes hard and prefers coffee. He lives in a very ordinary dwelling-house, and it is even stated that his vrouw starches and irons his dress-shirts, but this may only be surmise. At all events he does not allow these trifles to worry him, his renowned diplomacy being directed chiefly to the management of his cosmopolitan children, who are apt occasionally to wax troublesome and exceed the bounds of caution.

President Kruger's House.ToList

When a Government assumes a more or less aggressive attitude, or something tantamount, it is safe to predict that such a Government will encounter difficulties. It may be a good Government; but it will not be a successful one. The actions of any Government reflect upon the country, adversely or otherwise. In a country like the Transvaal, the Government is a weighty concern which does not so much consider the voice of the people as the preservation of its own individual sanctity. The presidential chair represents the universal criterion either for good or for evil, although it is not usually associated with evil. It practises the art of cabling — with Mr. Chamberlain for preference. The voice of the people is duly represented, but it is a very weak and halfhearted voice. There is not that hearty ring in it which is so marked when, for instance, a crowd of Englishmen greet their Queen. President Kruger represents the Transvaal burghers, and the requisitions which are published previous to the Presidential election are sufficient and convincing proof that he is a popular and highly respected man. These requisitions usually refer in a general way to the numerous difficulties through which Oom Paul has so ably piloted the country. According to such requisitions innumerable difficulties have assailed the poor country on all sides, and the general tone throughout would imply that they were insidious and uncalled for. The country had done nothing; the people had gone about their business innocently, and attended church regularly, and no thoughts of intrigue or anything resembling it had existed in their bosoms. Their desire was to govern the country honestly and with a view only to its prosperity, adopting precautions at the same time which would exclude the participation of foreigners — Englishmen, for example. They didn't believe in the English element; it was too dangerous. The President all the while tried to make out that he liked the English; but he didn't. Of course, a great Power like the Transvaal must keep up appearances. The German Emperor, for instance, doesn't say straight out that the English are a bad lot, and therefore Oom Paul must not display official ignorance by doing that which the German Emperor does not do. A man may not exactly be born a King, or a President, but he can learn a lot of useful little formalities by watching the other Kings and Presidents. It will be observed, therefore, that the Transvaal has all along been very docile and consequently very badly used. And because it has displayed the best and noblest qualities and on all occasions endeavoured to obviate friction with other people, it has been unjustly assailed and trampled upon.

Oom Paul is a very good man, but he kicks at the traces a great deal. He likes to go out of his way to find out what other people are saying about him, and he displays, moreover, another undesirable characteristic—he is suspicious. It is in the family; it is in the whole people. He is continually working himself up into the condition of a man whose highly-strung nerves convince him that the whole world is against him. He always imagined that everybody was working out plans of campaign by which it would be possible to annex the Transvaal to the British Empire. Fortunately there were other matters and other countries to consider, and if Oom Paul would just study a map of the world for a few weeks and reflect, he would probably find his position less irksome. But Oom Paul has a great deal to think about—he must think for the whole nation. The 'unfortunate affair which occurred after 1895' seems to trouble him a great deal. Despite the fact that the country was well paid for it, this incident seems fated to crop up at least every six months, and it will be handed down to generations untold, so that it may ever be kept green. It will be nurtured and well looked after, and the one regret will be that it does not bring in an annual income in proportion to the original amount.

President Kruger..ToList

The Boer's politics are summed up in the single word 'Defence.' He is not aggressive, but he is strong on Defence. Possession with him is ten points of the law — it is everything. Let the independence of his country be threatened, and he is at once a man of action. He figuratively converts his ploughshare into a sword, although the uses of that weapon are unknown to him. At the time of the Jameson Raid it may safely be asserted that there did not exist a single Boer — young or old — who was not in possession of a serviceable firearm and the full complement of ammunition. The Kantoors — i.e., the Government offices — were daily besieged by eager men as eager to possess themselves of the instruments and munitions of war. Every man was ready; farmers were no longer farmers, but soldiers, prepared to face the worst in the defence of their only love — their country.

CHAPTER VIToC

The Boer is not what one would call a sentimental person; he is practical in all his ways. If he sees a thunderstorm approaching, he does not go into raptures over the magnificence of the lightning; he watches that thunderstorm calmly and philosophically. And if he had anything to do with the order of the elements, he would have that thunderstorm come his way, and he would detain it exactly three days over his particular farm, so that the rain should leave a lasting impression upon his mealies and forage. The Boer likes wet weather, probably because he gets so little of it.

I have said that the Boer is practical in all things; he is even so in love. The old story concerning the 'opzit' candle may have applied in former days, but the Boer of the present day does not waste his time in any such fashion. He has probably become cognisant of the match-making methods practised by other nations, and he has, therefore, abandoned that affected by his forefathers. It is still a common thing, however, to see him astride a horse with a sleek skin and noble appearance and plenty of life in it, cantering gaily towards the residence of his beloved or intended. Sometimes, too, in order, perhaps, to add more lustre to his own appearance, he is to be seen suffering untold agony under the unyielding brim of a tall, white felt hat, trimmed with green veiling. He likes to look imposing, and so he gets under that hat. This in many instances may account for the restiveness of his steed, which is as yet unaccustomed to the weight of a person with such a grotesque headgear.

The Boer has several methods of courting. There is one thing he objects very strongly to, however—he doesn't like courting in a drawing-room; he prefers a dark and quiet corner on the veranda. Let us picture a little scene in this connection. Observe young Piet, dressed in his best Sunday suit, and wearing a worried look in addition, sitting on one end of a long form that stands on the veranda of the house; and observe also a fair young damsel, who has just been initiated into the art of doing her hair up on top, sitting on the other extreme end of that form. The night may be dark and only the stars visible, or the moon may be shining brightly overhead, casting shadows awry here and there, and endeavouring to catch a furtive glimpse of the lovers under cover of the veranda.

A painful silence takes the place of conversation at the outset, and young Piet occasionally coughs in an apologetic manner. When he does sum up sufficient courage, the moon has travelled a considerable distance; but then Piet is not so sentimental as to make any reference whatever to the moon.

'That's a fine horse your father has bought of Dirk Odendaal,' says Piet, in a tone which suggests that his new paper collar, purchased for the occasion, is choking him.

A two minutes' pause ensues.

'Ja! Piet,' agreeably assents the maiden after an interval which Piet reckons must be at least half an hour—and he has forgotten about the new horse altogether.

'Your father's oxen are looking well after the rain,' continues Piet some minutes later; and this time he has reduced the space between himself and the maiden by about three inches.

After the lapse of another few minutes, the maiden, who is evidently bashful, ventures again, 'Ja! Piet.'

Piet's eyes wander away across the open veldt in front of him, and gradually from the observation of kopjes, they wander upwards towards the pale moon; but, as has already been remarked, that luminary suggests no new theme in the mind of Piet.

'The last Nachtmaal was very good.'

With this he once more edges away from his end of the form and covers an additional three inches.

'Ja! Piet.'

Another person would have become exasperated at this stage, but not so Piet.

'The new minister preaches very well,' is followed up by an advance of three more inches.

'Ja, Piet!'

The form may be an inconveniently long one, and this naturally hampers Piet somewhat, because by the time he has covered half the distance, his stock of remarks may be exhausted. But he gets close up in time, by the exercise of perseverance, and when he is at last in a position to manipulate his left arm in connection with the maiden's waist, he does so with a sigh of relief.

'I think I love you a great deal,' is what he says when he has placed his arm to his satisfaction. The maiden whispers 'Ja, Piet!' and the thing is done.

But the young Boer does not attach so much importance to pleasant features and agreeable dispositions, as he does to the worldly standing of the lady's parents. If there is the slightest prospect of a handsome dowry in the shape of one or two farms, the inducement to enter into married bliss is, of course, greater than in the case of the young lady who merely brings with her a nice set of false teeth and a pleasant countenance. Young widows are in great demand throughout the country, because, as a rule, they are in possession of farms and stock which require the undivided attention of a responsible man, and that man must be a husband.

Such an instance occurred only the other day. This very fortunate young man, before his betrothal, could conveniently count his riches on the fingers of his left hand — in pence! But he is happy now, because he can bring in a load of wool every year with his own waggon and oxen, and talk to the merchant with all the swagger and assurance of a full-blown capitalist.

It must not be supposed that such occurrences are uncommon; they happen almost every week, which would seem to indicate that rich young widows are very plentiful.

In these latter days a Boer wedding is arranged on a very grand scale. No matter if the young couple reside fifty miles from the nearest town, they all come in to church to get fixed up. Friends and relations arrive, with great ostentation, in conveyances drawn by four, six, and sometimes eight, horses, the number depending on the wealth of the families. They come from far and near. You can see them coming to town when they are yet miles away across the veldt — that is, if the day is bright. The dresses of the women-folks flash gaily in the sun, and the old vrouw would not change places with the Queen of Holland as she proudly surveys her offspring seated around her in the wagonette. The old man presides unctuously at the ribbons, and he cracks his whip every now and then just to let his team know that he is there, and that he is a very capable person.

Dutch Church (Pretoria).ToList

The generality of weddings are uninteresting, but occasionally something unique is introduced. In the town of Harrismith a very long time ago, a transport-rider decided to take unto himself a fair partner. He was a practical sort of person, and in cases of this kind he did not believe in allowing business to become a secondary consideration. Transport-riding in those days paid very handsomely, and the intervention of side issues might have meant a serious loss. Accordingly, this particular gentleman (who had meantime been loading up coal) repaired to his tent-waggon at the appointed hour, and proceeded to attire himself in the conventional black suit. In order to economize time, he pulled his best clothes over his working garments, and hastily rubbing his face and hands with a coarse towel, he hurried towards the church. Within ten minutes he was back again loading up coal, his better half being occupied in preparing dinner.

The Dutch are not a musical nation, and for convincing proof it is only necessary to attend Divine service in any of their churches. Their rendition of psalm-tunes reminds me of A.K.H.B.'s story regarding the lonely Italian, who, passing the Iron Church in Edinburgh one Sunday morning while the congregation were engaged in praise, and on inquiring of the beadle 'What that horrible noise was?' remarked very sorrowfully, 'Then their God must have no ear for music' It is strange, nevertheless, that no matter how poor a Boer may be, he will have an organ in his house. There are instances innumerable where the only respectable piece of furniture in the house is an organ. It does not, of course, follow that every Boer is a musician, but it is a fact that nearly every Boer knows how to produce at least one tune, even if it is only the Volkslied or national anthem. They will come into the stores, and the first thing they do is to sit down at an organ and show people generally what they can do. In the meantime the English merchant and his clerks fume around and vow all sorts of things under their breath, but the indefatigable Boer knows nothing of all this, and he would not care if he did.

CHAPTER VIIToC

Besides the everlasting worry of keeping the English community in hand, the Boers have been visited by other plagues, such as rinderpest. In 1897 such a calamity befell them, and although the rich farmers did not suffer materially, the poorer class experienced reverses sufficient to discourage them for life. The mistake made was simply this (and it is characteristic of the Boers): every individual farmer and owner of stock exercised his own judgment throughout, and the most drastic results followed as a consequence. Temporary excitement naturally took the place of clear judgment. A man may be possessed of all his faculties and yet lack that knowledge which would save 95 per cent. of his cattle. The desire to save the cattle was there, but the farmers were too prone to accept the first method which turned up. Without even considering thoroughly the merits and demerits of any particular method, they rushed at it with the same prospect of success as might be attributed to a blind man going in search of the North Pole. Of course the system would 'either kill or cure.' That was how the majority of them put it. The veterinary surgeons received very little encouragement. If a Boer makes up his mind that his cattle are going to die, he likes to have all the honour of killing them himself, and he does not want any vet. about his place, propounding advanced theories which he does not understand. Added to this, it appears that when the disease first made its appearance in the country, certain vets, made themselves so ridiculous in the eyes of the farmers who invited them to inspect sick cattle, that distrust immediately took the place of suspicion, and confidence was never established.

Boer Cattle Farm Near Majuba.ToList

The farmers who managed to save a considerable number of cattle were not slow to make hay while the sun shone, and some of them may probably have turned up their noses at the mere mention of the Yukon goldfields. Prospecting for gold is a somewhat risky business, but the Boer looks upon transactions in salted oxen as eminently satisfactory, more especially where the buyer negotiates the risks. Nothing affords him more pleasure than to hand over twenty or thirty oxen, and receive in exchange twenty-five pounds per head. But, unlike the English problem, rinderpest is not always with the Boer.

In this connection there is a story to the effect that a certain Boer farmer discovered one day that his cattle had contracted a very serious disease, and he was advised by the Government vet., who happened to be passing that way, to inoculate immediately, and after the lapse of ten days to repeat the process. When the vet. returned a few weeks later he was surprised to learn that the majority of the cattle had died.

'But that was impossible if you acted on the instructions I gave you,' he said to the farmer.

'Ja!' answered the latter, 'that may be, but I didn't do what you told me; I only inoculated once.'

'And why didn't you do it a second time?' pursued the vet.

'Oh,' replied the Boer, 'because the vrouw said I hadn't to.'

Shooting Rinderpest Oxen.ToList

The Boer seldom does anything without first consulting his wife, and it is hinted that the wives made a very bad job of the rinderpest. The vrouw steers the ship. It is so when the whole family goes to town to make the half-yearly purchases. In the stores the husband will be found in deep and earnest conversation with his better half, relative perhaps to the quantity of barbed wire or coffee or wool-packs—anything and everything required at the time. All this would seem to point to a plain fact, namely, that the vrouw not only excels in physical proportions, but also in the matter of brains. There can be no doubt about the first mentioned, and there seems to be little question about the other as well. It is authoritatively stated that at the time of the Boer War the women were so bitter against the English that they spurred on the men to do things which they themselves deemed foolhardy. This anti-English feeling seems to have been intensified since then, and it is often jocularly remarked by Englishmen in the country that so long as an enemy makes things square with the womenfolk they need have no fear of the men. The women may have the reputation of knowing and doing more than the men, but they are certainly not thrifty. They are kind to travellers (provided they come on horseback and not on foot); but their kindness is too often spoiled by the dirt and general undesirability of the atmosphere within their dwellings. A traveller can appreciate a cup of coffee after a long ride; but he likes to have it in a clean dish, and it rather damps his ardour when he finds that he is expected to take the mud along with it.

Waggon On Pontoon Over River.ToList

In this connection there is still another story. This story is related by a commercial traveller, and in order to establish its authenticity it is only necessary to remark that it has been related by at least six different commercial travellers, and in every case the incident has occurred within the experience of each and all.

The commercial gentleman (no matter which one) having been overtaken on the road by a severe thunderstorm, and arriving at a spruit which he found he could not then cross with safety, put back to a small farmhouse near by. After much parley on both sides, the Boer who owned the place agreed to give the traveller and his driver shelter for the night, provided they would sleep in an outhouse, where the horses could also be put up. Being only too glad to obtain shelter of any sort, the traveller readily accepted the offer. At this point each traveller who has told the story breaks into a graphic description of how he passed the night, and how many rats he and the driver killed, and how much of his clothes they devoured, and how he couldn't sleep because of the presence of pigs and fowls in addition, which seemed to resent the invasion. Then comes the dawn of another day, and, which is more important (before its appearance), breakfast. A cloth was spread on a box in the mud-floor dwelling, and eggs and coffee placed thereon. The commercial was evidently expected to eat the eggs anyhow, so long as he did eat them; for there was nothing visible in the shape of a spoon. The Boer and his vrouw did not put in an appearance at breakfast, no doubt disdaining to look upon an Englishman any more than was absolutely necessary. He had almost concluded this rude and somewhat unsatisfactory meal when the vrouw entered. She was fat and dirty, and her clothing had apparently been renewed from time immemorial by much mending. She now rested her great hands on her hips, and calmly surveyed the English party and the breakfast-table for a few seconds. Then she spoke, in Dutch; but he understood — too well:

'Have you finished?'

'Yes,' he replied in the 'lands taal'; 'but surely you are in a very great hurry. I will pay you well for the food and shelter.'

'That's nothing,' continued the vrouw in a business-like tone; 'I only want the tablecloth so that I can get the bed made.'

CHAPTER VIIIToC

The Boer is a pious person, who prays to God when he wants rain, and forgets to pray when his mealie crop proves a success. Unlike other people, he does not believe in thanksgiving when he shells one hundred bags of mealies where he only expected twenty. He has no 'harvest home.' He simply stores his mealies until such time as he can bring them to town and obtain the best possible price. But let the rain stop away too long and the sun wither up his crops, and he is a very different man. In every Boer house there is a large Bible, and that Bible is systematically read and re-read when the fates are unkind. The very low class Boer is, of course, unable to read his Bible, but he takes it over to his nearest neighbour, whose education may not have been neglected to the same extent.

Boers Outspanned For Nachtmaal.ToList

The Boer journeys to town once every three months with his family in order to attend Divine Service. These occasions are known as Nachtmaal. He brings his waggon with him, and outspans on some open space within the town. When he cannot arrange for a room or rooms gratis, he sleeps in his tent waggon. He very seldom goes to a hotel, unless this course is absolutely necessary. If he does go to a hotel, he engages a room only, and dines alongside his waggon or else he goes to his particular storekeeper and indulges in sardines and sweet biscuits He is great on sardines, and his only regret perhaps, is that the tin is not edible also.

A Dutch Nachtmaal in the olden days was a sight quite equal to any Lord Mayor's show. The costumes were unique; but in the present day the womenfolk in particular have learned to ape the English, and the colours are therefore less conspicuous. Formerly the young ladies wore short dresses of many colours, and the display of white stockings was very general. The men appeared in black felt hats with huge brims, and frock-coats (most of them bordering on green) were the order of the day. Veldschoens of home manufacture were never wanting, but in these latter days veldschoens are regarded with contempt.

The man who probably suffers most at Nachtmaal-time is the organist, for organs are now regarded as indispensable. An organist is usually a man of a sensitive nature, and on such occasions his ideas of good music are apt to be completely demoralized. Nevertheless, he gets along as best he can, and even if he happens to be dragging a congregation numbering three hundred voices seven whole notes behind his instrument, he continues to suffer nobly and silently.

The services commence at 7 a.m., and continue throughout the day until 9.30 p.m. Baptisms occupy a few hours during the afternoon, and the most common names for youthful burghers are Gert, Barend, Paul, Piet, and such like. The Boers do not believe in departing from the time-honoured names of their forefathers. Piet suggests the immortal name of Piet Retief, and Paul—well, there is Oom Paul.

Before the marriage ceremony can be performed in a Dutch Reformed Church, the minister must satisfy himself that the contracting parties have previously been confirmed. Great preparation for the confirmation is engaged in by the young people a week before Nachtmaal Sunday, on which day, in presence of the whole congregation, they are received into the bosom of the Church.

The Boer is very conscientious in the matter of religion. For instance, should he be on bad terms with any of his friends or relations, he will not attend Divine Service. He argues that a man who is not at peace with his fellow-men cannot hope for reconciliation with his God until the difference has been amicably settled.

It may be observed that the order of service in a Dutch Church is very similar to that in vogue in a country church in Scotland. The minutest details have much in common, but perhaps I had better not enlarge upon such a coincidence. Before each service the men-folk linger in front of the church door, with their hands stuck deep down in their pockets and the inevitable pipe between their teeth. They talk about almost everything except religion—the crops, their petty difficulties with Kaffirs, the last hailstorm and the havoc it worked, and so on. The Boers never enter into theological arguments. Each and all place implicit faith in the Scriptural teachings, and they take for granted everything from the beginning to the end of their Bibles. Consequently the teachings of Scripture are not very firmly impressed on their minds.

When the organ begins to peal forth the voluntary, the worshippers troop into their seats. During the choral part of the service the congregation remain seated, and they rise when the minister prays. The elderly gentlemen very promptly go to sleep when the text is given out, and they lean back in their respective corners with the full assurance that they will not be disturbed for at least an hour. Occasionally they may be gently aroused by their wives or children, whose supply of sweets has been exhausted. By the way, every Boer in the country has one particular weakness, and that is a desire after sweets. The young men recklessly walk into a store whenever they come to town, and devote a portion of their capital to the purchase of 'Dutch mottoes,' to which the ladies are very partial. The elderly men are not so particular in this respect.

When the benediction is about to be pronounced, there is a general scramble after hats, and the last Amen has scarcely been uttered when there is a rush for the doors. It seems to amount to a sort of competition as to who will be first in the street.

It may be interesting to pause for a moment and look at the collections. The poorer classes besiege the stores on Saturday with anxious inquiries for 'stickeys,' i.e., threepenny-pieces. To a poor man with a large family of church-goers this matter of church collections is a serious business unless he can get four mites out of a shilling, as coppers are not used in the Transvaal; but I have known men of good standing inquire as eagerly for the despised threepenny-piece. When special collections are called for, in aid of a new organ fund, for instance, the results are rather surprising. In one instance the combined special collections on a Nachtmaal Sunday amounted to a little over £500, with a congregation of only 400. This points to the fact that there is money enough in the country, and it only requires a church collection to prove it.

It is to be regretted that the Boer does not devote a little more attention to the education of his children. If there happens to be a school anywhere near his farm, he does not mind taking advantage of this with a view to 'teaching the young idea how to shoot'; but perhaps he takes too literal a view of this adage. His chief care is to see that his boys are taught to shoot straight, and he does not attach so much importance as he might to the three R's. The Boer who can afford such luxuries engages a tutor for his children, but tutors are mostly of the English persuasion. They have not yet learned to appreciate the language of the country, and this constitutes a serious barrier. Again, one does not expect much of a country school, and the majority of the men who preside over these institutions in the Dutch Republics are there simply because they can obtain no more lucrative an occupation. A number of Free State farmers invariably 'trek' to Natal with their families and stock during the winter months, and this affords an opportunity for placing the children at more advanced schools; but then again the objection is serious—the masters are English.

Bloemfontein.ToList

In the town of Bloemfontein, Orange Free State, where the Volks-raad thunders forth its mighty convictions, there is a model Young Ladies' College. It seems that one day recently the members of the Raad found themselves in want of debatable motions, and it fell to the lot of one of their number to save the situation. That member directed the attention of his brethren to a certain question affecting the proper conduct of the Young Ladies' College aforesaid. It had come to his knowledge that the Principal of the College had grant-ed, to certain of the pupils who desired it, permission to pray to Almighty God in the English language. The member forcibly con-tended that this lamentable state of affairs should not exist, but that every pupil in the College should be compelled to pray to God in the language of the country! A general discussion followed, but it was ultimately allowed that this matter did not come within the jurisdiction of that Raad.

CHAPTER IXToC

Every town has its Landdrost, and every town has its Landdrost's clerk. Usually the clerk does all the work, and the Landdrost, in his capacity of chief magistrate, passes all the sentences and issues all the instructions. But, then, Landdrosts, as a rule, are very agreeable people, possibly because they are educated and intelligent men, and have nothing in common with the Boer.

I have one particular Landdrost in my mind as I write. He was a dear old man, but he was dead against Kaffirs and natives generally. His father had been killed by Kaffirs, and this fact probably rankled in his bosom and ruled his judgments to a great extent. When he wanted to show a little bit of leniency, as, for instance, after an extraordinarily good breakfast, he would bind the culprit over to serve in his own kitchen for a period of one year without remuneration. But he never did get a native to serve the full time, because the native preferred to break the law once more and go to 'tronk' instead. Hard work was not in his line.

He is dead now, poor man! but he was a regular type of a Landdrost. He lived a very quiet life, and the brunt of the work fell to the lot of the ever-willing and conscientious clerk, which arrangement allowed the Landdrost sufficient leisure to attend to a somewhat large garden. There were fruit trees in that garden which in the fruit season incited every boy in town to deeds of valour, the said deeds consisting in being able to carry away as much fruit as possible without being caught in the act. For the Landdrost exercised a watchful eye over that fruit. It was currently reported, however, that his was the first garden to be literally left desolate before the season had far advanced, and it was usually his misfortune to be deprived of his fruit just after he had retired for the night, after having prowled about with an empty gun in his hand from sunset till late in the evening. It was even reported that one evening, after the old man had retired as usual, a certain person who had a strong predilection for other people's fruit approached the Landdrost's garden with a handcart and a lantern, and assisted himself freely before taking his departure.

In conclusion, and as an illustration of the moral tendencies of young Boers generally, I shall now quote a little scene which was written some time ago for another purpose.

In a mealie-field close to a certain farm, which shall be nameless, a curious scene was being witnessed by a very stout Dutch lady. She was standing at the edge of the field. Above her head myriads of locusts floated in a darkening mass. The mealie stalks were only a foot or so high, but the locusts knew that they were green, and therefore good to eat, so they hovered around. The mealies were in rows, and between these rows galloped half-a-dozen horses carrying half-a-dozen very raw natives. The latter were making such a hideous noise, that it seemed to point to remarkable staying powers on the part of the locusts, inasmuch as they still persisted in trying to gain a footing. But the Kaffirs cantered their steeds faster, and the noise waxed more hideous, and the fat vrouw continued to urge them to renewed and increased effort. Round the edges of the patch four or five Kaffir women walked, each at a different point, and each in possession of a five-gallon empty paraffin tin and a stick, with which to strengthen and augment the noisy defence. The locusts were reinforced every minute, and they made repeated and determined efforts to sample the young mealies, but the horsemen and the paraffin tins were too much for them.

A small white boy was standing near the fat lady, watching the proceedings with a critical eye. His dress was very primitive, and his home-made veldschoens were very large, but he was a healthy-looking boy.

'Ma,' he said at length, looking up into the fat lady's face, 'I see something.'

This was rather a peculiar remark to make, because undoubtedly he must see something, not being blind.

'Yes,' returned his 'ma,' without taking her eyes off the mealie patch, 'what do you see, son?'

'I won't tell you, ma.'

'Ma' paid no particular attention to this decision on the part of her small son, but he continued to look into his 'ma's' face as if uncertain about something.

'Ma, I won't tell you what I see,' he continued, coming up closer to the stout lady and catching hold of her hand.

'Why won't you tell me, son?' asked 'ma,' looking down affectionately upon the white head of her boy.

'Not until you promise me something, ma.'

'Well, what must I promise you?'

The boy hesitated for a minute before replying. He had apparently grave doubts as to whether 'ma' would concede even if he did ask her.

'Ma, I want to shoot Witbooi with my gun.'

Witbooi was a Kaffir umfaan, who had no particular liking for his young Baas.

'I can't promise you that until your pa comes home, Gert,' said his 'ma,' patting him lovingly on the head, and at the same time lending her critical eye to the mealie business.

The boy left his mother's side and walked away a few yards, evidently disgusted with unsympathetic 'mas.' Then, apparently changing his mind, he ran towards her again, and clung to her dress, meantime looking up in her face.

'I'll tell you, ma — I'll tell you,' he said laughingly.

'That's a good boy,' said 'ma,' again patting him on the head.

'I see waggons coming; that's it!' exclaimed the boy, running away playfully, and observing with evident satisfaction the look of surprise on his mother's face, as if it atoned somewhat for the disappointment regarding the fate of Witbooi.